LATIN Q

IN

PARIS

A 2024 TRAVEL GUIDE ON A JOURNEY THROUGH THE SOUL OF PARIS

MICHAEL SMART

This BOOK belongs to

____

____

From:

____

Signature/Date:

____

TABLE OF CONTENTS

INTRODUCTION

Welcome to Paris's fascinating Latin Quarter, where history, intelligence, and creative flare meet together. Nestled on the left side of the Seine River, the Latin Quarter, or *"Quartier Latin"* in French, is a charming area that has long been a hub of intellectual and artistic activity.

History

The Latin Quarter's name alludes to the medieval era when Latin was the language of research and instruction. This area has witnessed the ebb and flow of ages, and its small, cobblestone lanes tell stories of academic passion and bohemian flair. As you walk along these streets, you'll feel as if you're in a living history, with the voices of great philosophers, artists, and students echoing from every corner.

Educational Hub

The prestigious Sorbonne University, a beacon of academic achievement since the 12th century, is located in the heart of the Latin Quarter. The Collège de France, another venerable institution, adds to the area's intellectual vigor. The presence of these prominent educational institutions has given the Latin Quarter a reputation as a shelter for intellectuals and thinkers, influencing the neighborhood's very identity.

Architectural marvels

Aside from its scholastic relevance, the Latin Quarter is a visual treat for architectural fans. The streets are lined with structures from many epochs, including medieval, Renaissance, and more. Among the most visible landmarks is the Panthéon, a neoclassical masterpiece that holds the remains of notable French individuals. Wander through the Luxembourg Gardens, where the grandeur of French gardening unfolds, providing a peaceful respite from the city buzz.

Cultural Haven

As you wander the Latin Quarter's convoluted alleyways, you'll come across lovely bookstores, art galleries, and small cafes that have inspired authors and artists for years. The ancient Shakespeare and Company bookstore, a literary refuge, welcomes you to enter a world of words and imagination. The quarter's bohemian vibe is mirrored in its vibrant nightlife, with pubs and entertainment establishments inviting both residents and visitors.

Practicality Meets Pleasure

This guide will help you discover the secrets of the Latin Quarter. The Latin Quarter has something for everyone, whether you're a history buff, an art aficionado, a life student, or just an inquisitive tourist. In the next chapters, we'll go over the practical parts of your stay, including transportation, lodging, and food alternatives. You'll also learn about the must-see sites, museums, and hidden jewels that distinguish the Latin Quarter from the rest of the City of Light.

Take a trip through time and culture as we peel back the layers of the Latin Quarter, encouraging you to taste the intellectual history, embrace the artistic energy, and create your unique moments in this enchanted corner of Paris. ***Welcome to the Latin Quarter!***

CHAPTER 1

GETTING TO THE LATIN QUARTER

Beginning your journey to the Latin Quarter is the first step in immersing yourself in Paris' rich tapestry of history and culture. This major area on the left side of the Seine River is easily accessible, with several transit alternatives and effective navigational aids.

1. Arrive in Paris

The most popular entrance point for foreign passengers is Paris Charles de Gaulle Airport (CDG), which is roughly 25 kilometers northeast of the city center. Alternatively, Paris Orly Airport (ORY), located about 13 kilometers south of the city, serves as another significant international gateway. There are several modes of transportation available from these airports to the Latin Quarter.

2. Airport transfers

- **Taxis and ridesharing services** are easily accessible at both airports. While taxis provide easy door-to-door service, ridesharing services are a more cost-effective choice.

- **Airport Shuttle Services:** Several shuttle services connect Paris' airports to major hotels and attractive neighborhoods. These shared trips are a cost-effective method to get to your destination.

- **Public Transportation:** Efficient rail service connects both airports to the city core. The RER B train departs from CDG and stops at significant stations like as Saint-Michel-Notre-Dame, which is centrally located in the Latin Quarter. Orly is connected with the Orlyval light rail system and associated trains.

3. Navigating Paris via Metro

Once in the city, the Paris Métro (subway) system is a great way to get around. The Latin Quarter has many metro stations, including Cluny-La Sorbonne, Saint-Michel-Notre-Dame, and Odéon. The metro network is broad, dependable, and an inexpensive way to explore different sections of Paris.

4. Bus services

Paris has an extensive bus network, with multiple routes connecting different regions of the city, including the Latin Quarter. Buses are a lovely way to travel, enabling you to take in the scenery as you wind your way through the quaint neighborhoods.

5. Walking and Bike

When you're in the center of Paris, exploring by foot or by bicycle is a great alternative. The Latin Quarter's small alleyways and old sites are best explored at a leisurely pace. Many routes are pedestrian-friendly, while bike-sharing programs offer a more environmentally friendly mode of transportation.

6. Navigation Aids

- **Maps and Mobile Apps:** Carry a thorough map of Paris or use your Smartphone's navigation software. Apps like Google Maps, Citymapper, and Paris Métro can assist you in planning your trips, whether you're walking, cycling, or taking public transit.

- **Signage:** Paris is well-marked, with clear signs for metro stations, bus stops, and major attractions. Follow the signs and don't be afraid to ask locals for directions; they are typically delighted to help.

Navigating the Latin Quarter is more than simply a practical trek; it also serves as an introduction to the city's beauty. As you walk through the streets and bridges, you'll feel the history beneath your feet and the vivid energy that marks this famous Parisian district. So, whether you come by air, rail, or bus, let the experience begin as you enter the Latin Quarter's enchanted embrace.

CHAPTER 2

ACCOMMODATIONS IN AND AROUND

Choosing the appropriate lodging sets the tone for your whole trip, and the Latin

Quarter in Paris has a wide variety of alternatives to suit every budget and desire. From historic hotels to quaint guesthouses and low-cost hostels, the Latin Quarter offers a fascinating variety of options, each adding to the particular appeal of your stay.

1. Luxury Retreats: Historic Hotels

The Latin Quarter is home to numerous luxury hotels that flawlessly combine modern comfort with the grandeur of ancient architecture. These restaurants provide an immersive experience, allowing customers to enter the past while enjoying modern comforts.

- **Hôtel Lutetia:** This landmark hotel on the left bank of the Seine is a historical treasure. Since 1910, the Hôtel Lutetia has entertained intellectuals, artists, and dignitaries. With Art Deco decor and Michelin-starred food, it provides a genuinely luxurious experience.

- **Hôtel La Villa Saint-Germain:** Nestled in the heart of Saint-Germain-des-Prés, near the Latin Quarter, this boutique hotel mixes Parisian style with individual service. Its contemporary accommodations and closeness to cultural attractions make it a popular choice among discriminating tourists.

2. Cozy Retreats: Charming Guest Houses

For those looking for a more private and customized experience, guesthouses in and around the Latin Quarter offer a welcoming ambiance. These beautiful rooms frequently have a distinctive design and a personal touch.

- **Le Petit Belloy:** Located on a quiet street, Le Petit Belloy is a quaint hotel that embodies the character of the Latin Quarter. Its modest accommodations and dedicated staff provide a welcoming atmosphere, making it popular with individuals who want a more private environment.

- **Hotel Henriette:** Despite being a hotel, Hotel Henriette radiates the ambiance of a guest home. Each room is uniquely created with a combination of historical and contemporary elements, providing guests with a beautiful and comfortable getaway.

3. Budget-Friendly Accommodations: Hostels and Affordable Hotels

For budget-conscious tourists, the Latin Quarter features several hostels and inexpensive hotels that offer a comfortable stay without breaking the bank. These alternatives are great for students, travelers, and anybody wishing to discover Paris on a budget.

- **Young and Happy Hostel**: Located in the center of the Latin Quarter, this hostel offers affordable lodging in a youthful and dynamic setting. It's a popular choice among solitary travelers and backpackers looking for a communal setting.

- **Hotel Minerve:** Hotel Minerve, located near the Panthéon, provides cheap accommodations in a strategic position. The no-frills approach appeals to budget tourists by offering a clean and pleasant place to relax after a day of seeing.

Accommodation Options for various budgets

1. Luxury travelers

- For a sumptuous experience, stay at legendary luxury hotels such as Hôtel Lutetia or Hôtel La Villa Saint-Germain.

- Consider boutique hotels that combine luxury and individual service.

2. Mid-Range Comfort

- Look at mid-range hotels like Hôtel des Grands Hommes, which strike a compromise between comfort and expense.

- Look for well-reviewed guesthouses like Le Petit Belloy for a comfortable stay at a reasonable price.

3. Budget-Friendly Options

- For a comfortable and affordable stay, choose cheap hotels like Hotel Minerve.

- Young and Happy Hostel is a sociable and cheap housing alternative.

Practical Tips for Booking

1. Book in Advance: Especially during high travel seasons, reserving your accommodations in advance assures availability and may result in lower rates.

2. Consider Location: Choose lodging near metro stations or key monuments for easy access to the Latin Quarter and other attractions.

3. Read Reviews: Use review platforms to assess the experiences of prior guests. This includes information about the quality of service, amenities, and general satisfaction.

4. Investigate Package Deals: Some hotels offer package deals that include lodging, food, or other goodies, delivering excellent value for money.

Whether you like the richness of historic hotels, the intimacy of guesthouses, or the low-cost atmosphere of hostels, the Latin Quarter caters to every taste and budget. When you settle into your selected hotel, you're not simply getting a place to sleep; you're also immersing yourself in the particular atmosphere of one of Paris' most interesting districts. From opulent getaways to tiny hideaways, your home away from home awaits in the heart of the Latin Quarter.

CHAPTER 3

EXPLORING THE STREETS

The charming Latin Quarter is located in the center of Paris, where the Seine River flows elegantly through the city. As you walk through its small, cobblestone lanes, you begin on a trip through time, surrounded by distinctive architecture that tells stories of centuries past. From the majestic Notre Dame Cathedral to the picturesque lanes that run through the area, every aspect of the Latin Quarter exudes history, culture, and an innate Parisian fascination.

1. Characteristic Architecture

The Latin Quarter is a living canvas of architectural styles, with each structure conveying a tale about its age. As you walk through its streets, you'll see a seamless combination of medieval, Renaissance, and Haussmannian architecture, forming a beautiful tapestry that symbolizes the neighborhood's long history.

- **Medieval Marvels:** The Latin Quarter is home to several medieval buildings with timbered facades, arched doors, and tiny lanes. One of the best examples is the Cluny Museum (Musée de Cluny), which is situated in a 15th-century chateau of Gothic and Romanesque architecture.

- **Renaissance Gems:** The district is known for its Renaissance architecture, particularly the lovely Place de la Sorbonne. The Sorbonne University, built in the 13th century, is a perfect combination of medieval and Renaissance architecture, with a tranquil courtyard hidden away from the busy streets.

- **Haussmannian Elegance:** In the nineteenth century, Baron Haussmann renovated Paris, including the Latin Quarter. While the region kept much of its medieval beauty, Haussmannian boulevards gave a sense of grandeur. Boulevard

Saint-Michel, a lively boulevard, illustrates this era with its broad avenues and exquisite architecture.

2. Famous Streets and Alleys

As you explore the Latin Quarter, you'll come across iconic streets and secret lanes that reflect the spirit of Parisian life. Each artery has its distinct appeal, allowing you to explore art, history, and the dynamic atmosphere of the area.

- **Street Saint-Germain:** This famous street is a cultural hotspot, studded with booksellers, cafés, and designer boutiques. Stroll down its large sidewalks, where intellectuals and artists previously congregated in the famed cafés, adding to the neighborhood's bohemian vibe.

- **Rue Mouffetard:** This vibrant market street is a sensory pleasure. It is cobbled and lined with a variety of businesses, bakeries, and fresh food markets, capturing the feel of a Parisian market street. The Place de la Contrescarpe, at its higher end, is a beautiful area where you can relax and people-watch.

- **Rue de la Huchette:** This small medieval lane takes you back in time. Rue de la Huchette, which is lined with restaurants, jazz clubs, and souvenir stores, has a vibrant atmosphere. It's a popular spot for both residents and visitors, especially in the evening when the street comes alive with music and conversation.

- **Saint-André-des-Arts:** This lovely street connects Boulevard Saint-Germain to the Seine and is lined with art galleries, tiny theaters, and cafés. It's perfect for taking strolls, admiring street art, and discovering independent stores.

3. Hidden Alleys: Revealing Secret Charms

The Latin Quarter's appeal stems not just from its vast boulevards, but also from the secret lanes and tunnels waiting to be found. These peaceful areas show a more personal aspect to the community, where time appears to stand still.

- **Cour du Commerce Saint-André:** This medieval tunnel is tucked away behind Boulevard Saint-Germain and contains a wealth of history. It captures the essence of the Latin Quarter, with its stores, bistros, and theaters. Café Procope, one of Paris' oldest cafes, is located in this lovely courtyard.

- **Route Saint-Michel:** This covered route, which connects Rue Saint-André-des-Arts and Boulevard Saint-Michel, emanates old-world elegance. It is lined with businesses offering books, antiques, and souvenirs and offers a quiet escape from the hectic streets.

- **Rue Galande:** This small, ancient lane with timbered buildings and cobblestones seems like stepping back in time. It leads to the lovely Place de la Contrescarpe, providing a look into the Latin Quarter's medieval fabric.

Tips For Exploring the Streets

1. Take Your Time: The beauty of the Latin Quarter is in the details. Slow down, wander around the streets, and let yourself be enchanted by the architectural marvels and hidden treasures.

2. Explore beyond the Main Streets: Venture into tiny alleys and tunnels to uncover true Parisian experiences and delightful spots that may go unnoticed.

3. Visit at Different Times: The mood of the Latin Quarter changes throughout the day. Experience the bustling bustle during the day and the seductive allure as the evening approaches.

4. Engage with Locals: Start talks with locals, whether at a café or a little business. They may provide observations, recommendations, or tales about the community.

Every stride through the alleys of the Latin Quarter is an opportunity to uncover the complexities of Parisian culture and history. From the grandeur of Boulevard Saint-Germain to the intimate appeal of secret lanes, this area encourages you to immerse yourself in the wonder of its streets, where every corner tells a tale and every step exposes the City of Light's everlasting fascination.

CHAPTER 4

CULTURAL AND EDUCATIONAL INSTITUTIONS

The Latin Quarter in Paris is more than just a historic area; it is a thriving center of intellectual and artistic activity. This region, steeped in centuries of scholastic and creative pursuits, is home to famous educational institutions and cultural landmarks that have helped form the city's intellectual landscape. From the famous Sorbonne University to the intriguing Cluny Museum, the Latin Quarter provides a diverse range of activities for anyone looking to immerse themselves in Parisian culture and knowledge.

1. Sorbonne University is a beacon of learning

The Sorbonne University, located in the heart of the Latin Quarter, is renowned for its academic quality and intellectual endeavor. The Sorbonne, founded in the 12th century, has had a significant impact on Paris and the world's intellectual history. Its famous main structure, with its majestic architecture and medieval courtyard, exemplifies centuries of research.

Visitors may discover the Sorbonne's rich history by engaging in guided tours that uncover the mysteries of its halls, libraries, and lecture rooms. The Sorbonne not only provides academic programs, but also sponsors cultural events, conferences, and seminars that add to the intellectual life of the Latin Quarter.

2. Collège de France: A Center for Interdisciplinary Exploration

The Collège de France, located adjacent to the Sorbonne, offers another degree of intellectual distinction to the Latin Quarter. This school, founded in the 16th century, operates on a unique principle: instructors are not constrained by a set curriculum and are free to pick their fields of study. This technique encourages interdisciplinary inquiry and allows scholars to delve into a variety of topics.

The Collège de France welcomes the public to its lectures, making it an accessible environment for people interested in cutting-edge research and thought-provoking ideas. The Latin Quarter's image as an intellectual sanctuary stems from the institution's devotion to intellectual freedom, which has attracted some of the brightest minds.

3. The Cluny Museum (Musée de Cluny) offers a journey through medieval art

The Cluny Museum is a fascinating journey through medieval Europe for art and history enthusiasts. The museum, which is housed in the Hôtel de Cluny, a medieval residence, displays an impressive collection of Middle Ages relics, sculptures, and illuminated manuscripts.

One of the museum's attractions is the Lady and the Unicorn tapestry series, which is known for its meticulous craftsmanship and symbolic narrative. Visitors may also wander around the museum's medieval gardens, which take visitors back in time to an age of chivalry and artistic beauty. The Cluny Museum, with its well-organized displays, adds to the cultural diversity of the Latin Quarter.

4. Shakespeare and Co.

Despite not being a regular academic institution, Shakespeare & Company is a cultural monument in its own right. This famous English-language bookstore has been a shelter for writers, poets, and readers since its inception in 1951. The bookshop, located near Notre-Dame Cathedral, has a pleasant ambiance that is a treasure trove of literature, drawing literary fans from all over the world.

Shakespeare and Company has a unique history of providing authors with a place to stay in exchange for helping out at the shop, which pays respect to Sylvia Beach's original Shakespeare and Company in the 1920s. The bookshop continues to hold literary events, book readings, and meetings, cultivating a creative community in the heart of the Latin Quarter.

5. Café de Flore and Les Deux Magots

While not typical educational institutions, the Café de Flore and Les Deux Magots are notable literary cafés that have contributed significantly to the Latin Quarter's cultural fabric. These businesses on Boulevard Saint-Germain were frequented by prominent writers and intellectuals like Jean-Paul Sartre, Simone de Beauvoir, and Albert Camus.

Café de Flore and Les Deux Magots were formerly intellectual hotspots where literary conversations and debates thrived. Today, they emit a literary vibe, drawing tourists looking to drink up the environment that has inspired generations of intellectuals.

Tips For Cultural Exploration

1. Attend Public Lectures: Check the timetables at Sorbonne University and Collège de France for public lectures and activities. Attending these seminars gives information about current research and intellectual conversations.

2. Engage with Art: Take your time studying the exhibitions of the Cluny Museum, admiring the skill of medieval painters. The Lady and Unicorn tapestries are a must-see.

3. Visit Literary Cafés: Spend the afternoon drinking coffee at Café de Flore or Les Deux Magots, immersed in the literary legacy that pervades these historic establishments.

4. Explore Independent Bookstores: In addition to Shakespeare and Company, go into smaller bookstores in the Latin Quarter. You can come upon undiscovered literary gems and unexpected finds.

The cultural and educational institutions of the Latin Quarter combine academic discovery with artistic appreciation in a cohesive manner. Whether you're digging into medieval history at the Cluny Museum, attending a lecture at the Sorbonne, or immersing yourself in the literary ambiance of legendary cafés, each experience adds to the lively cultural mosaic of this ancient Paris district.

CHAPTER 5

LANDMARKS & MONUMENTS

The Latin Quarter, located in the center of Paris, combines history and contemporary and reveals its treasures via renowned structures and monuments. Each edifice offers a tale, weaving together centuries of creative accomplishment, cultural progress, and architectural genius. From the majestic majesty of the Panthéon to the ageless charm of the Luxembourg Gardens, the Latin Quarter is a living museum of Parisian grace and history.

1. Panthéon

The Panthéon, located atop Montagne Sainte-Geneviève, is a neoclassical masterpiece that compels attention and devotion. Originally established as a cathedral devoted to Saint Geneviève, Paris' patron saint, it was later converted into a secular tomb during the French Revolution. The Panthéon presently holds the remains of notable French individuals, such as Voltaire, Rousseau, and Marie Curie.

The massive façade, complete with Corinthian columns and a towering dome, exemplifies the architectural grandeur of the Enlightenment period. The spacious space is filled with natural light, generating a sense of solemnity and wonder. The Panthéon serves as a tribute to France's intellectual and political past, allowing visitors to consider the achievements of its revered personalities.

2. Notre-Dame Cathedral is a symbol of Gothic grandeur

While being restored following the tragic fire in 2019, Notre-Dame Cathedral remains a living monument of Gothic architecture and spiritual significance. Its ornate façade, embellished with flying buttresses, gargoyles, and carved saints, fascinates those who see it. The cathedral's interior, with its rose windows and lofty nave, conveys a feeling of celestial transcendence.

Despite being temporarily restricted to the public during repair operations, Notre Dame's façade continues to inspire adoration. The meticulously sculpted features reflect a story of medieval workmanship and religious devotion, reminding us of the cathedral's long-standing status as a cultural and architectural landmark.

3. The Luxembourg Gardens are a tranquil oasis

Away from the rush and bustle of city streets, the Luxembourg Gardens provide a tranquil escape that mixes natural beauty with traditional grandeur. These finely planted gardens, designed in the 17th century at the request of Marie de' Medici, surround the Luxembourg Palace, which currently houses the French Senate.

The gardens' attractiveness stems from its beautiful combination of formal French design and English-style landscaping. Visitors may walk along tree-lined paths, see statues and fountains, and rest by the octagonal pond. The Luxembourg Gardens exemplify the Latin Quarter's elegance and sophistication, offering a calm getaway for both inhabitants and tourists.

4. Saint-Étienne-du-Mont

Nestled near the Panthéon, the Saint-Étienne-du-Mont church is a masterpiece that combines Gothic and Renaissance architectural styles. The church's exterior has beautiful stone carvings and a spectacular rood screen, while the inside boasts breathtaking stained glass windows and a great choir. The mixture of architectural styles in Saint-Étienne-du-Mont illustrates the changing creative inclinations that have defined the Latin Quarter throughout the ages.

One of the church's most outstanding features is the stunning spiral staircase that leads to the choir loft. This architectural masterpiece attracts tourists seeking spiritual tranquility as well as respect for bygone ages' skills.

5. Place de la Sorbonne

Surrounded by ancient buildings and bounded by the Sorbonne University, the Place de la Sorbonne is a plaza steeped in intellectual heritage. The Sorbonne's main structure, with its renowned dome, dominates the Piazza, providing an atmosphere that combines intellectual aspiration and architectural splendor. The place comes alive with students, teachers, and intellectuals, adding to the Latin Quarter's scholarly atmosphere.

Tips For Exploring Landmarks and Monuments

1. Consider attending a guided tour to learn more about the history and significance of buildings like the Panthéon and Notre-Dame Cathedral.

2. Seasonal Beauty: Visit the Luxembourg Gardens in different seasons to see the changing hues of the flora and feel the distinct beauty that each season provides.

3. Attend a Service: If feasible, attend a service or performance at Saint-Étienne-du-Mont to experience the old church's acoustics and spiritual environment.

4. Cafe Culture: Take a leisurely café break near these sites, drink up the ambiance, and watch the world go by.

The Latin Quarter's buildings and monuments are more than just architectural wonders; they are also living witnesses to Paris's evolving history. Whether you're experiencing the spiritual grandeur of Notre Dame or meandering through the tranquil Luxembourg Gardens, each site provides an insight into the cultural diversity that distinguishes this historic area. Every stone, statue, and garden in the Latin Quarter has a tale that captivates and inspires visitors.

CHAPTER 6

MUSEUMS AND ART GALLERIES

The Latin Quarter, located in the center of Paris, showcases its cultural assets through a variety of museums and art galleries, all of which contribute to the district's reputation as a sanctuary for creative and intellectual pursuits. From the medieval splendors of the Cluny Museum to the bohemian vibe of Shakespeare and Company, the Latin Quarter provides a rich tapestry of experiences for both art lovers and curious visitors.

1. Musée de Cluny (Cluny Museum)

Tucked away in the Latin Quarter, the Musée de Cluny, better known as the National Museum of the Middle Ages, enables tourists to go back in time to medieval Europe. The museum is housed in the Hôtel de Cluny, a 15th-century chateau, and has an outstanding collection of antiquities, tapestries, sculptures, and illuminated manuscripts.

One of the highlights is the enchanting "Lady and the Unicorn" tapestry series, which is known for its superb craftsmanship and symbolic narrative. The museum's themed displays cover the medieval period, providing insight into everyday living, religious rituals, and creative triumphs of the time. The museum's calm medieval garden enhances the immersive experience, making Musée de Cluny a must-see for history and art fans.

2. Shakespeare and Company's Literary Sanctuary and Cultural Hub

Shakespeare and Company, while not a standard museum, is an independent cultural institution. Established in 1951 by George Whitman, this famed English-language bookstore has provided a haven for writers, poets, and readers alike. The bookshop, located near Notre-Dame Cathedral, is not just a book lover's paradise, but also a thriving cultural hub that conducts literary events, book readings, and conversations.

The atmosphere of the original Shakespeare and Company, founded by Sylvia Beach in the 1920s and frequented by literary luminaries such as Ernest Hemingway and James Joyce, remains on in the current location. Visitors may immerse themselves in the comfortable atmosphere, surrounded by bookshelves, and take part in the Latin Quarter's rich literary legacy.

3. The Musée Curie traces the legacy of Marie Curie

The Musée Curie, located in the historic Curie Institute, honors the pioneering work of Nobel Prize-winning scientist Marie Curie and her husband Pierre Curie. The museum takes visitors on a fascinating trip through the history of radioactivity and the Curies' scientific accomplishments. Visitors may enter the laboratory where radium was discovered, see original equipment and tools used by the Curies, and learn about their pioneering research.

The Musée Curie provides a unique chance to interact with the Latin Quarter's scientific past by highlighting the convergence of art, culture, and important discoveries.

4. The Institute of the Arab World serves as a cultural bridge

The Institut du Monde Arabe, located along the Seine River, is a stunning architectural masterpiece built by Jean Nouvel. Beyond its stunning appearance, the institution functions as a cultural bridge, encouraging understanding and appreciation for the Arab world. The museum features a wide variety of exhibitions, including art, antiquities, and multimedia displays that delve into the Arab world's rich history, art, and traditions.

The panoramic terrace offers stunning views of Paris and the Notre Dame Cathedral. The Institut du Monde Arabe demonstrates the Latin Quarter's dedication to promoting cultural interaction and understanding.

Tips for visiting museums and art galleries

1. Check Opening Hours: Before arranging your visit, be sure to check the museums and galleries' opening hours, since they may change. Some universities provide nighttime hours on certain days.

2. Guided Tours: Consider taking a guided tour to have a better understanding of the exhibits and the historical background behind them.

3. Café Culture: Many museums and galleries feature on-site cafes or neighboring eateries. Take a break for a leisurely coffee or snack to process your experiences.

4. Special Exhibits & Events: Stay up to date on special exhibits, events, and talks taking place in Latin Quarter museums and galleries. These can provide distinct perspectives and experiences.

The Latin Quarter's museums and art galleries entice visitors with the promise of intellectual stimulation, artistic appreciation, and cultural immersion. Whether you're discovering the ancient treasures of Musée de Cluny, the literary refuge of Shakespeare and Company, or the scientific history of Musée Curie, each institution adds to the complex tapestry that distinguishes this historic Parisian region. The Latin Quarter brings art and history together, encouraging you to go on a thrilling journey through the past.

CHAPTER 7

CAFÉS AND RESTAURANTS

The Latin Quarter, located in the center of Paris, where history and culture intersect, serves up culinary delights through a profusion of attractive cafés and restaurants. From the ancient literary cafés on Boulevard Saint-Germain to the small bistros nestled along cobblestone lanes, the Latin Quarter provides a culinary experience that reflects the city's diversity and elegance.

1. Café de Flore

Café de Flore, located on Boulevard Saint-Germain, is a cultural institution that has maintained its ageless elegance since the nineteenth century. The café, frequented by literary luminaries such as Jean-Paul Sartre and Simone de Beauvoir, has a bohemian appeal reminiscent of the intellectual enthusiasm of the past.

Guests may enjoy a leisurely coffee or a delicious lunch on the renowned terrace, witnessing the ebb and flow of Parisian life. During the colder months, the interior, which is decorated in crimson velvet and wood, provides a comfortable hideaway. Café de Flore not only provides delicious food, but it is also a living testament to the Latin Quarter's rich literary legacy.

2. Les Deux Magots

Les Deux Magots, located next to Café de Flore, has the same ancient street and literary history. Since the 19th century, philosophers, authors, and painters have frequented this historic café. The café's name, "The Two Figurines," comes from the two Chinese sculptures that originally graced the premises.

Les Deux Magots, with its Art Deco decor and patio overlooking Place Saint-Germain-des-Prés, remains popular with both locals and visitors. The menu features a beautiful selection of French classics, delivering a gourmet experience rich in history and elegance.

3. La Sorbonne: Student-Friendly Eateries

The Latin Quarter, home to the prestigious Sorbonne University, is peppered with student-friendly restaurants catering to a diverse audience. Rue de la Huchette, in particular, is noted for its bustling environment and a variety of eateries that provide affordable alternatives. From crêperies to various cuisines, these restaurants capture the neighborhood's young vibrancy and cosmopolitan flare.

Students and residents frequently congregate at these businesses, resulting in a vibrant atmosphere that spills onto the streets. The broad combination of cuisines and reasonable menus make this neighborhood a gastronomic playground for people looking for a variety of eating experiences.

4. Le Procope

Le Procope was founded in 1686 and is one of Paris' oldest continually functioning cafés. Located in the center of the Latin Quarter, this venerable restaurant has welcomed intellectuals including Voltaire, Rousseau, and Benjamin Franklin. Its magnificent décor, complete with antique mirrors and vintage furnishings, transports diners to the golden age of French cuisine.

Le Procope's menu includes a variety of classic French meals, allowing customers to experience the gastronomic legacy that has distinguished the Latin Quarter for generations. The café's historical significance, paired with its culinary offerings, make it a must-see for anybody looking for a taste of Parisian history.

5. L'Ambroisie

For those who appreciate gastronomic quality, L'Ambroisie is a shining example of culinary talent in the heart of the Latin Quarter. This Michelin-starred restaurant on Île Saint-Louis provides a sophisticated dining experience in a historic setting.

Led by Chef Bernard Pacaud, L'Ambroisie is known for its painstaking attention to detail and steadfast devotion to excellence. The menu features traditional French cuisine elevated to the level of high art. Diners may luxuriate in superb cuisine made with precision while enjoying the attractive environment of Île Saint-Louis.

Tips for Culinary Exploration

1. Explore Side Streets: Venture beyond the main boulevards to find hidden gems such as lovely bistros and small eateries nestled in narrow alleys.

2. Try Local Specialties: To experience the region's original flavors, try classic French delicacies like escargot, coq au vin, and crème brûlée.

3. Dine Al Fresco: When the weather permits, choose outside to sit at cafés and restaurants to enjoy the lively atmosphere and gorgeous vistas.

4. Culinary Events: To enhance your eating experience, check out the Latin Quarter's culinary events, food festivals, and special deals.

The Latin Quarter's cafés and restaurants are more than just places to eat; they are extensions of Parisian history, culture, and innovation. From drinking coffee in literary cafés where intellectual conversation takes place to indulging in Michelin-starred cuisine, every culinary experience in this historic area is a sensory journey—a celebration of the sensations that define the City of Light.

CHAPTER 8

THE ENCHANTING NIGHTLIFE

As the sun sets over the gorgeous alleyways of the Latin Quarter, a new vitality emerges, converting this ancient quarter into a thriving nightlife destination. From vibrant jazz clubs to secluded wine cellars, the Latin Quarter provides a diverse range of nighttime experiences, enabling both locals and visitors to immerse themselves in the captivating world of Parisian after-hours entertainment.

1. Jazz and blues at Le Caveau de la Huchette

Le Caveau de la Huchette, located in the heart of the Latin Quarter, is a famed jazz and blues club that seems like stepping back in time. This historic Parisian institution, housed in a 16th-century cellar, has been around since the 1940s. Le Caveau de la Huchette's stone walls, arches, and cozy atmosphere convey an old-world elegance that compliments its musical offerings.

Visitors may sway to the beat of live jazz and blues bands, immersing themselves in the vibrant environment that has captivated jazz fans for decades. The club's ageless charm makes it an essential stop for anyone looking for a genuine jazz experience in the center of Paris.

2. Latin Rhythms at Le Latin

Le Latin, located on Rue du Faubourg Saint-Jacques, is a bustling nightclub that reflects the Latin Quarter's passionate atmosphere. This club's unique blend of Latin music, from salsa to reggaeton, entices dancers to the floor. The vivid energy and throbbing beats create an atmosphere in which guests may dance the night away, enjoying the synthesis of many rhythms.

The club frequently holds themed evenings, which draw a mixed population of residents and visitors. Whether you're an experienced dancer or a beginner looking to learn, Le Latin provides an immersive and vibrant nightlife experience that encapsulates the essence of the Latin Quarter.

3. Literary Evenings at Shakespeare and Company

While Shakespeare & Company is best known as a bookstore during the day, it morphs into a one-of-a-kind literary venue at night. The bookshop occasionally sponsors evening activities, such as book readings, poetry recitals, and conversations. These events offer an intimate and intellectual nightlife experience, allowing participants to discuss literature in a casual and social atmosphere.

As the lights lower and the shelves throw shadows, Shakespeare & Company transforms into a literary refuge where words come alive after sunset. The programs frequently draw a varied crowd of book enthusiasts, resulting in a comfortable and intellectually interesting environment.

4. Atmospheric Cocktails at Little Red Door

Little Red Door on Rue Charlot provides a classy and personal drink experience that goes beyond the ordinary. This speakeasy-style bar features experienced mixologists who create unique and visually appealing cocktails. The softly lighted atmosphere and plush chairs provide a sophisticated elegance, making it an excellent choice for a relaxing evening.

The ever-changing menu at Little Red Door highlights the craft of mixology, with fresh ingredients and innovative taste combinations. Each drink is a meticulously created work of art, pleasing both the palate and the sight. The bar's dedication to inventiveness and quality makes it one of the top locations for cocktail connoisseurs in the Latin Quarter.

5. Bohemian Vibes at Le Saint Régis

Le Saint Régis, located along the Seine River, provides a relaxed and bohemian atmosphere that reflects the character of the Latin Quarter. This bar's outside patio overlooks the river and Notre Dame Cathedral, making it ideal for a relaxing night out. The intimate environment, complete with vintage decor, contributes to the establishment's distinct character.

Patrons may enjoy a variety of beverages, including artisan beers and exquisite wines while taking in the beautiful environment of the Seine. Le Saint Régis is a favorite of both residents and tourists, offering a relaxing and attractive environment for an amazing night in the Latin Quarter.

Tips for a Night Out in the Latin Quarter

1. Explore Side Streets: Look beyond the main boulevards to find hidden gems like tiny wine bars and eccentric taverns nestled in picturesque lanes.

2. Check Event Calendars: Stay up to date on special events, live performances, and themed evenings at various Latin Quarter venues for a well-curated nightlife experience.

3. Embrace Late Nights: Parisians frequently enjoy leisurely evenings, with numerous establishments being open till the early morning. Accept the slow pace and enjoy the night.

4. Combine Culinary and Nightlife: Many of the Latin Quarter's cafés and restaurants change into

bustling bars in the evening, allowing customers to go smoothly from dining to dancing.

The Latin Quarter's nightlife offers a diverse range of events, from soulful jazz to bustling dance floors and small literary meetings. Whether you're sipping drinks in a chic speakeasy or dancing to Latin beats in a lively club, the Latin Quarter's after-hours culture invites you to experience the enchantment of Parisian nights, where every corner offers the promise of an unforgettable evening.

CHAPTER 9

SHOP & STROLL

Nestled on the Left Bank of the Seine River, Paris' Latin Quarter is a refuge for intellectuals and history buffs, as well as a great shopping destination. From quaint shops on cobblestone alleyways to legendary bookstores and modern concept stores, the Latin Quarter provides a broad range of shopping experiences that reflect the district's bohemian attitude and rich cultural past.

1. Book Lovers' Paradise

For literary fans, no trip to the Latin Quarter is complete without a stop at the famed Shakespeare & Company. Founded in 1951 by George Whitman, this famed English-language bookstore has attracted writers, poets, and book lovers from all over the world. The shelves are stocked with a carefully picked collection of books, ranging from classic literature to modern works.

Shakespeare & Company is more than simply a bookstore; it is a literary sanctuary with a distinct heritage. The shop frequently holds literary events, book readings, and conversations, allowing visitors to connect with the Latin Quarter's thriving literary community.

2. Bohemian Chic: Concept Stores on the Rue du Cherche-Midi

Rue du Cherche-Midi, with its tree-lined walkways and trendy stores, is a sanctuary for fashion lovers looking for distinctive and quirky treasures. This boulevard is home to various concept boutiques that combine boho charm with Parisian grace. From avant-garde apparel to meticulously designed home décor, these boutiques provide a unique shopping experience.

Explore the stores on Rue du Cherche-Midi to find a mix of known French designers and young talent. The environment is calm, enabling customers to peruse their time and discover one-of-a-kind objects that embody Parisian elegance.

3. Artistic Treasures: Rue de la Huchette and Saint-Michel Market

Rue de la Huchette, a bustling and historic street, is recognized for its diverse selection of boutiques, cafés, and souvenir shops. The street radiates bohemian appeal, making it an excellent destination for visitors looking for creative treasures and one-of-a-kind mementos. From handcrafted jewelry to vintage posters, the stores on Rue de la Huchette provide a diverse selection of things that represent the district's artistic culture.

The nearby Saint-Michel Market enhances the shopping experience. This open-air market on the Seine River has kiosks offering antiques, literature, and artwork. It's a great spot to explore on weekends, with opportunities to discover hidden gems and enjoy the picturesque riverbank surroundings.

4. Luxury Shopping on the Boulevard Saint-Germain

Thoroughfare Saint-Germain, a wide thoroughfare running through the center of the Latin Quarter, is a luxury retail hotspot. Famous fashion houses and upmarket retailers cover the streets, providing a refined shopping experience. Boulevard Saint-Germain caters to individuals who appreciate timeless elegance in everything from high-end apparel to fine jewelry and accessories.

Take a stroll down the avenue, admiring landmark stores and designer boutiques that embody Parisian elegance. The ambiance is elegant, and the window displays are a visual feast for fashion enthusiasts.

5. Vintage Finds at Marché Mouffetard

For a taste of Parisian street market culture, visit Marché Mouffetard, one of the city's oldest and most vibrant marketplaces. This market, located on Rue Mouffetard, has a diverse selection of vendors selling fresh vegetables, cheeses, flowers, and vintage items. It's a gathering spot for both residents and visitors looking for high-quality foods and one-of-a-kind things.

Wander around the market's small lanes, smelling the scent of freshly made bread and enjoying the vibrant ambiance. Marché Mouffetard is more than simply a shopping destination; it's an immersive experience that encapsulates everyday life in the Latin Quarter.

Tips for Shopping in the Latin Quarter

1. Explore Side Streets: Venture into the tight alleyways and side streets to locate secret boutiques and one-of-a-kind items that may be off the major thoroughfares.

2. Visit Markets: Open-air markets, such as Marché Mouffetard, provide a combination of fresh vegetables, vintage wares, and a glimpse into local life.

3. Engage with artists: Many stores in the Latin Quarter are run by individual artists and designers. Engage with them to learn about the craftsmanship of the things on exhibit.

4. Combine Culture and Shopping: Plan your shopping plan to incorporate visits to cultural monuments and attractions, ensuring a well-rounded experience in the region.

The Latin Quarter's commercial culture reflects its varied and creative character. Whether you're looking for rare books at Shakespeare and Company, browsing concept stores on Rue du Cherche-Midi, or immersing yourself in the bustling markets, every shopping trip in this ancient quarter is a voyage through Paris' cultural tapestry.

CHAPTER 10

FESTIVALS & CELEBRATIONS

The Latin Quarter, located in the center of Paris, comes alive with a rich tapestry of events and festivals that represent the city's cultural vitality and historical significance. The Latin Quarter has a variety of activities throughout the year, ranging from literary conferences and music festivals to vivid street fairs that attract both locals and visitors.

1. Festival de la Musique

Every year on June 21st, the streets of the Latin Quarter come alive with the joyous sounds of Fête de la Musique, a national music festival. This exciting festival transforms the neighborhood into an open-air stage where amateur and professional musicians demonstrate their skills. The Latin Quarter transforms into a musical melting pot, with jazz, classical, rock, and electronic sounds all represented.

Cafés, squares, and even impromptu street acts add to the celebratory mood. Visitors may meander around the cobblestone streets, enjoying the different musical performances and basking in the social spirit that distinguishes Fête de la Musique.

2. Nuit Blanche: A Night of Creative Revelry

Nuit Blanche, which translates as "White Night," is an annual event that illuminates Paris' streets at night. This cultural event, usually held in October, invites contemporary artists to produce installations, performances, and exhibitions that turn public places into immersive works of art. The Latin Quarter, with its ancient structures and meandering lanes, serves as a canvas for these inventive emotions.

From lighted sculptures to interactive installations, Nuit Blanche allows visitors to see the city in a new light, both literally and symbolically. The squares and prominent sites of the Latin Quarter serve as a unique background for this charming festival, which brings together art and nightlife.

3. Salon du livre (Paris Book Fair)

For bibliophiles and literary fans, the Salon du Livre, or Paris Book Fair, is a highly anticipated event. This annual literary event, generally held in the spring, brings together authors, publishers, and book enthusiasts from all over the world. The Latin Quarter, with its ancient bookshops and literary tradition, forms an essential component of this cultural event.

Visitors to the event can attend book signings, panel discussions, and speeches by well-known writers. The Latin Quarter's booksellers frequently hold related activities, resulting in a literary ambiance that pervades the region during Salon du Livre.

4. Fête de Saint-Germain-des-Prés

Fête de la Saint-Germain-des-Prés is a delightful local event that honors the historical and cultural history of Saint-Germain-des-Prés, a district in the Latin Quarter. This festival, which is typically held in May, includes a range of events such as art exhibitions, live concerts, and gastronomic experiences.

The event celebrates Saint-Germain-des-Prés' distinct character, which is noted for its literary cafés, art galleries, and lively environment. During the celebrations, visitors may participate in guided tours, watch concerts, and learn about the cultural heritage of this historic Parisian neighborhood.

5. The Ancient Music Festival

La Fête de la Musique Ancienne, held in the Latin Quarter, is a unique festival for classical and ancient music enthusiasts. Held yearly, this festival presents performances of medieval, Renaissance, and Baroque music in historic locations such as churches and cultural monuments.

Audiences may immerse themselves in the sounds of millennia ago, discovering the beauty and intricacy of old musical traditions. The Latin Quarter's ancient churches and cultural institutions provide a fitting setting for this one-of-a-kind celebration of musical history.

Tips to Enjoy Events and Festivals

1. Check Event Calendars: To learn about forthcoming events and festivals in the Latin Quarter, consult local event calendars and official websites.

2. Plan: Some festivals may draw enormous crowds, so it's best to plan and come early, especially for events with limited seating or capacity.

3. Engage with Locals: Festivals are an excellent opportunity to meet locals and other travelers. Strike up a discussion, participate in the festivities, and enjoy the communal spirit.

4. Explore Beyond Main Events: While attending large events, stroll through the surrounding streets and venues to find hidden treasures and smaller gatherings that add to the joyful ambiance.

The Latin Quarter's events and festivals create a rich tapestry of culture, art, and community. Whether you're immersed in the musical exuberance of Fête de la Musique or exploring the literary delights of Salon du Livre, each festival provides a fresh perspective on the vibrant atmosphere of this ancient Parisian neighborhood.

CHAPTER 11

PRACTICAL TIPS FOR VISITORS

A visit to Paris's Latin Quarter is a pleasant trip that brings history, culture, and modernity together. To make the most of your visit to this renowned region, it's a good idea to come prepared with useful suggestions. From comprehending currencies and payment options to navigating linguistic intricacies and ensuring your safety, here's how to have a smooth and pleasurable stay.

Currency & Payment

1. **The official currency of France is the Euro (€).** It's a good idea to have extra cash on hand for little transactions because not all locations accept credit cards for modest sums.

2. **Credit and debit cards** are frequently accepted throughout the Latin Quarter, particularly in restaurants, hotels, and bigger retailers. Visa and MasterCard are the most popular, however, it's a good idea to notify your bank about your vacation dates to minimize problems with card transactions.

3. **ATMs:** ATMs are widely available around the Latin Quarter, allowing you to withdraw cash as required. Check your bank's overseas withdrawal costs and currency conversion rates.

4. **Contactless Payments:** Many Paris shops, particularly those in the Latin Quarter, now accept contactless payments. If your card offers this capability, it might be a quick method to settle bills.

Language

1. **French is the official language:** While many individuals in the Latin Quarter, particularly those in the tourism business, speak English, it is appreciated if you try to utilize simple French phrases. Locals are frequently kind to visitors who try to converse in their language.

2. **Common phrases:**

Hello: Bonjour (Bohn-Zhoor)

Thank you: Merci (mehr-see).

Please: (seel voo pleh)

Excuse me/Pardon: Excusez-moi (ex-kew-zay mwah)

Goodbye: Au revoir (oh reh-vwahr).

3. **Linguistic Apps:** For rapid translations and linguistic aid, try Duolingo or Google Translate. These can be useful for understanding menus and signs.

4. **Politeness Matters:** French culture places a high value on politeness. Remember to say "Bonjour" when entering a store or establishment and "Au revoir" while leaving. Simple acts of courtesy go a long way toward leaving a good impression.

Safety

1. **General Safety:** While the Latin Quarter is a generally safe place, you should always be careful of your surroundings. Keep a watch on your stuff, especially in busy locations, and be wary of pickpockets, especially in tourist hotspots.

2. **Emergency Numbers:** In France, the emergency number is 112 for all services. For police help, phone 17, and for medical situations, dial 15.

3. **Consider purchasing travel insurance** that protects against medical crises, trip cancellations, and lost or stolen possessions. This gives additional piece of mind during your vacation.

4. **Health precautions:** Before flying to Paris, make sure you have all of the essential vaccines. Learn about the locations of nearby hospitals and pharmacies.

Public transportation

1. **Metro System:** The Paris Metro provides an effective and easy means to get about the city, including the Latin Quarter. Purchase a rechargeable Navigo card to enjoy unlimited rides within specific zones.

2. **Walking:** The Latin Quarter is recognized for its attractive streets and ancient landmarks, making it an ideal place to explore on foot. Wear comfortable shoes, since you may be walking through cobblestone streets and lovely lanes.

3. **Bicycles and Scooters:** Paris has a bike-sharing system called Vélib', and electric scooters are also available for short trips. If you want to utilize these kinds of transportation, become familiar with the traffic regulations.

Cultural Etiquette

1. **Dining Customs:** When entering a restaurant, it is traditional to greet with "Bonjour" and leave with "Au revoir". Tipping is often included in the bill; nevertheless, rounding up or leaving a modest amount is appreciated.

2. **Café Culture:** In cafés, particularly in the Latin Quarter, it is customary to linger and enjoy your coffee or meal at leisure. Do not rush, since the French like taking their time at cafés.

3. While there is no specific dress code, Parisians often dress cleanly and beautifully. It's best to avoid too casual dress, especially if you're going to fancy restaurants or cultural events.

Weather Considerations

1. **Seasonal Variations:** Paris has distinct seasons. Summers can be warm, while winters can be cold. Check the weather prediction before your journey and pack appropriately.

2. **Rain Gear:** Paris is known for its occasional rain. Bring a small umbrella and a waterproof jacket to keep dry during unexpected showers.

3. **Comfortable Layers:** Because temperatures fluctuate throughout the day, layering is a reasonable solution. This lets you adapt to shifting weather conditions.

Armed with these practical suggestions, you'll be able to confidently traverse the lovely alleys of the Latin Quarter. These suggestions ensure a seamless and delightful experience in one of Paris' most renowned districts, whether you're relishing the flavors of local food, learning about the district's rich history, or taking part in vivid events.

CHAPTER 12

DAY TRIP DELIGHTS

While the Latin Quarter in Paris is a remarkable destination in and of itself, the surrounding areas provide appealing day-trip choices for travelers to see France's various landscapes and cultural riches. Here are some recommended day trips that guarantee a lovely respite from the hustle and bustle of the metropolis.

1. Versailles Palace & Gardens:

- The distance from the Latin Quarter is approximately 17 kilometers (10 miles).

- Highlights: Visit the sumptuous Palace of Versailles, a UNESCO World Heritage site renowned for its ornate architecture and rich history. Explore the carefully groomed grounds, complete with fountains and statues, to feel the grandeur of the French monarchy.

2. Giverny:

- The distance from the Latin Quarter is approximately 75 kilometers (47 miles).

- Highlights: Explore the lovely environment that inspired Impressionist painter Claude Monet. Visit Monet's residence and gardens at Giverny, where you may walk amid the famed water lilies and colorful flower beds that served as inspiration for his works.

3. Château de Fontainebleau:

- The distance from the Latin Quarter is approximately 55 kilometers (34 miles).

- Highlights: Explore the magnificence of the Château de Fontainebleau, a former royal house with a rich history reaching back to the 12th century. Explore the elaborate rooms, expansive courtyards, and lovely woodland that surround this architectural masterpiece.

4. Champagne region:

- The distance from the Latin Quarter is approximately 150 kilometers (93 miles).

- Highlights: Enjoy a day of sparkling elegance in the Champagne area. Visit renowned champagne houses, such as Moët & Chandon and Veuve Clicquot, to see the cellars, learn about the champagne-making process, and taste delicious samples.

5. Mont Saint Michel:

- The distance from the Latin Quarter is approximately 360 kilometers (224 miles).

- Highlights: Take a beautiful tour to the famed Mont Saint-Michel, a medieval monastery located on a rocky island in Normandy. Admire the gorgeous architecture, winding lanes, and breathtaking views of the surrounding bay.

6. Disneyland Paris:

- The distance from the Latin Quarter is around 40 kilometers (25 miles).

- Highlights: For a day of family enjoyment, visit Disneyland Paris. In the mesmerizing world of fairytales and adventure, you may experience the charm of your favorite Disney characters, exciting rides, and stunning parades.

These recommended day visits provide a varied range of experiences, including regal magnificence, creative inspiration, and natural beauty. Whether you choose to see the opulent halls of Versailles, stroll through Monet's garden in Giverny, or marvel at the medieval splendors of Mont Saint-Michel, each day excursion promises to bring new aspects to your Parisian vacation.

CONCLUSION

As the sun sets behind the Latin Quarter's old buildings and cobblestone streets, it becomes clear that this charming region is more than just a physical place; it is a living tapestry woven with threads of history, culture, and vivid life. The Latin Quarter, with its famed literary cafés and secret bookstores, as well as the vibrant festivals that resound through its lanes, exemplifies Paris' lasting appeal.

Whether you're savoring the tastes of a local restaurant, discovering the winding alleyways rich with centuries of history, or dancing to the beat of a jazz-filled night, the Latin Quarter calls with a distinct appeal that grabs the heart of every visitor. It is a location where the voices of philosophers, artists, and students reverberate, resulting in a timeless environment.

Every turn in the Latin Quarter promises discovery, and each step exposes a different aspect of the city's personality. As you leave this literary and cultural sanctuary, you take with you not just recollections of historic buildings, but also the spirit of Paris itself—an unforgettable stamp that assures the Latin Quarter will be a lasting chapter in your journey of adventure and amazement.

DESTINATION(S)	DATE(S)

Currency Exchange

1 ____ = ____ ____ 1 ____ = ____ ____

1 ____ = ____ ____ 1 ____ = ____ ____

TRANSPORTATION					
depart	arrive	date&time	type	carrier	confirmation

ACCOMODATION					
name	location	dates	type	address	contact

PRE-TRAVEL CHECKLIST	
☐	☐
☐	☐
☐	☐
☐	☐
☐	☐

DESTINATION(S)	DATE(S)

Currency Exchange

1 ____ = ____ ____ 1 ____ = ____ ____

1 ____ = ____ ____ 1 ____ = ____ ____

TRANSPORTATION					
depart	arrive	date&time	type	carrier	confirmation

ACCOMODATION					
name	location	dates	type	address	contact

PRE-TRAVEL CHECKLIST	
☐	☐
☐	☐
☐	☐
☐	☐
☐	☐

DESTINATION(S)	DATE(S)

Currency Exchange

1 ____ = ____ ____ 1 ____ = ____ ____

1 ____ = ____ ____ 1 ____ = ____ ____

TRANSPORTATION					
depart	arrive	date&time	type	carrier	confirmation

ACCOMODATION					
name	location	dates	type	address	contact

PRE-TRAVEL CHECKLIST	
☐	☐
☐	☐
☐	☐
☐	☐
☐	☐

DESTINATION(S)	DATE(S)

Currency Exchange

1 ____ = ____ ____ 1 ____ = ____ ____

1 ____ = ____ ____ 1 ____ = ____ ____

TRANSPORTATION					
depart	arrive	date&time	type	carrier	confirmation

ACCOMODATION					
name	location	dates	type	address	contact

PRE-TRAVEL CHECKLIST	
☐	☐
☐	☐
☐	☐
☐	☐
☐	☐

TRIP At A Glance

DESTINATION(S)	DATE(S)

Currency Exchange

1 ____ = ____ ______ 1 ____ = ____ ______

1 ____ = ____ ______ 1 ____ = ____ ______

TRANSPORTATION					
depart	arrive	date&time	type	carrier	confirmation

ACCOMODATION					
name	location	dates	type	address	contact

PRE-TRAVEL CHECKLIST	
☐	☐
☐	☐
☐	☐
☐	☐
☐	☐

DESTINATION(S)	DATE(S)

Currency Exchange

1 ____ = ____ ____ 1 ____ = ____ ____

1 ____ = ____ ____ 1 ____ = ____ ____

TRANSPORTATION					
depart	arrive	date&time	type	carrier	confirmation

ACCOMODATION					
name	location	dates	type	address	contact

PRE-TRAVEL CHECKLIST	
☐	☐
☐	☐
☐	☐
☐	☐
☐	☐

TRIP *At A Glance*

DESTINATION(S)	DATE(S)

Currency Exchange

1 ____ = ____ ____ 1 ____ = ____ ____

1 ____ = ____ ____ 1 ____ = ____ ____

TRANSPORTATION					
depart	arrive	date&time	type	carrier	confirmation

ACCOMODATION					
name	location	dates	type	address	contact

PRE-TRAVEL CHECKLIST	
☐	☐
☐	☐
☐	☐
☐	☐
☐	☐

NOTES

NOTES

NOTES

NOTES

NOTES

NOTES

NOTES

Made in the USA
Columbia, SC
18 April 2024